How to Develop a Profitable Trading Strategy

I0476085

Why You Should Do the Opposite of
What the Majority of Traders is Trying to
Do

translated from the German original

Heikin Ashi Trader

DAO PRESS

Imprint

First edition, January 2020

Published by:

Dao Press is an imprint of Splendid Island, Ltd.

Scanbox 05927

Ehrenbergstrasse 16a

10245 Berlin - Deutschland

Tablle of Contents

Part 1: Do the Opposite of What the Crowd of Traders is Trying to Do!

1. What Traders Can Learn from Automatic Trading Systems

Traders go to the stock market for no other reason than to collect points, tics and pips. As much as possible and as fast as possible. Everything else is pastime and useless analysis. Traders therefore need a method, a system that does exactly that: accumulating small profits permanently, which eventually add up to a considerable plus in the account.

Therefore, trading is therefore not about analyzing the financial markets and trying to predict future prices. As a rule, most traders fail with this kind of approach. They want to understand the market. My experience is rather that one cannot understand the way financial markets behave. Too many actors with different intentions are at the same time in them and push the price arbitrarily back and forth. The first step towards success comes therefore with the insight that traders cannot understand the behavior of the market. As a result, they cannot analyze it and certainly not predict it. I know an army of analysts is trying this repeatedly. They merely satisfy the needs of the public for explanations, be they of a fundamental or technical nature.

These explanatory models may work for a while. Eventually the time will come that those models start to produce losses. The result is, of course, that the trader will be frustrated and will try to analyze his past trades (again!). On the other hand, even worse, he will try to optimize his system. In the worst case, he will be looking for a new strategy from which he finally hopes the desired success might come. In this spiral of searching for the perfect strategy, many traders get in. Repeatedly they put their hope in something new. In addition, they are always disappointed again. Although they might have success occasionally, a new unlucky blow will soon replace it.

Most financial markets that I know are so efficient that it seems to be almost impossible to beat them. They force the trader to surrender. Therefore, many people give up again and then spread the rumor that you cannot make money on the stock market. I too had gone this painful way and was close to giving up. Only when I started to look at automated trading systems has led to look at trading in a very different kind of way. After years of vainly trying to get a grip on my trading through technical analysis, I now learned a much sober way of looking at stock market transactions.

If you are afraid that you will have to go this excessively, I ask you for some trust and patience. You do not have to switch your trading to automatic. This is not the purpose of this book. I would like to use a few concrete examples to show what I have learned from dealing with automatic trading. Moreover, my hope is that you also have the opportunity to look at trading in a completely different   way.

Nowadays there are already many trading platforms, which also allow the nonprofessional to perform simple back testing. A back test is a method by which the trader can check a certain trading idea for its robustness. With this software, he can thus perform a backward-directed test. This shows him in seconds how he would have cut off if he had traded this idea in the past years. He not only gets the results of these thousands of trades that the computer simulates for him. It also provides a thorough statistical analysis of this test.

Those data shows him in detail whether it was at all worthwhile to have traded this trading idea. I hope it speaks for itself that a trading idea, which has not worked in the past ten years, is likely not to work in the next ten years (there are exceptions).

If, on the other hand, the trader has an idea that has worked very well over the past ten years, then it has good chances to repeat this over the next ten years. There is no guarantee here, but the chances are in any case better if the back test is positive.

Having such information is important to me before a trader starts working with a trading idea at all. If the trader knows black on white that he has a stable and successful strategy, he will be able to trade it with more confidence. This is, of course, especially important when things do not go so well. In addition, such periods occur - as we all know - repeatedly. For this reason, I would like to encourage those readers who are not (yet) familiar with automatic trading systems to try it. I can assure them it is worth it. I too, for a long time, barred myself against it. First, because I am not a big light in math anyway. Second, because I do not understand much of software and are already glad when the programs, which are installed on my PC, run smoothly. I think this is true for most people.

However, I was wrong to block myself from dealing with automatic trading systems because I was denied important insights into how trading really worked. I would have been just too happy to have such data when I started scalping futures 15 years ago. My trading career would have been different, and the learning curve would have been faster.

In addition, there are now excellent programs available to the nonprofessional who can serve every child. You can, as it were, test certain strategies without having any knowledge of programming. There is nothing to prevent the use of automated trading, even if you never intend to entrust real money to such a program.

In addition, should it not work out, your broker is at your disposal to help you. Do not forget: the task of a broker is to support you in order that you can trade. After all, that is the way he earns his money. The employees of your broker company will be glad to help you, should you have problems with a back test or with setting up a template. I have used the services of my broker several times in this regard, and he has always helped me freely and free of charge. Every time I learned, something more about automated trading.

It would be even better, of course, if you have someone in your circle of acquaintances who is familiar with such programs. If you know such a person, I recommend you to invite him to dinner or do him any other pleasure. This investment is worthwhile. Alternatively, you can of course join a trader club or a group on the Internet that deals with this topic. These topics are discussed in detail in countless forums. You will find real professionals here and there, who will gladly help you if you have any questions.

As I said, I am not here to convince you of the advantages of automated trading systems. There are, as well as the disadvantages. You can still enter your trades manually and decide when you want to trade or not. I would simply like to point out the advantages that the engagement with automatic trading also brings with it for the so-called "manual trader".

The trader, who runs his trading business completely manually, can learn an infinite amount of traders who act automatically. For example, he can learn to think about trading in a much more objective way and therefore act more rationally. Above all, he might learn less how "the markets work", but how trading works! The reader will immediately understand what I mean by reading more.

2. Do the Opposite of What is in the Trading Books

Success in any business often occurs when you do the opposite of what the mass does. I think that speaks for itself. However, most traders I know act against this maxim. They want to hear from the so-called "successful traders" what they are supposed to do. They then try to imitate these strategies or even try to trade in the same way as "the successful trader". As a rule, this does not lead to the desired success.

I will now look at some classic recommendations from the trading literature in this book and do just the opposite of what these well-meant advice suggest. I am not saying the reader should do this as well. I do not give any recommendations anyway. Everyone is responsible for his own trading and his own luck. However, I hope that thanks to this thought experiment; the reader will come up with new ideas. Perhaps it will enable him to look at his own trading in a different way.

Assertion 1: Cut Your Losses and Let Your Profits Run

The first assertion or classic recommendation that I would like to attack is: "cut your losses and let your profits run". Every trader knows this sentence. You can find it like a mantra in almost every trading book. At first glance, there is not much to be said against it. It certainly makes sense to everyone that in order to make money on the stock exchange; a trader should lose as little as possible and again as much as possible.

However, I put this sentence into question, especially when dealing with short-term trading or day trading. If you look at the background of this saying, you will find that it comes from a very specific corner. Namely from the corner of the trend follower. Trend followers are traders, whose philosophy is that they always see stocks and markets in long-term or medium long-term trends.

As a result, these traders will try to follow the trend. If, to put it simply, they have identified a trend in a stock or in a market, they will buy it. They then try to stay in this market as long as possible until their system gives some signal that the trend is over. Once they are in a proper trend, they earn money, of course. That is the reason why they say: let your profits run. Therefore, they follow the trend as long as it exists. This is clear rational behavior. Unfortunately, this method does not always work. Sometimes a trend follower buys a market that has moved in a certain direction and then experiences that he stops to move. The trader has a position, but this does not make him any money. He does not lose anything, but neither wins anything. He just loses his time.

In addition, of course, the opposite of what the trend follower is hoping for happens too. No sooner has he bought, the market turns, and the position begins to lose money. That is why the first part of the recommendation is to limit losses. As soon as a position goes into the loss, the trend follower must close it and take the smallest possible loss. He must therefore be willing to take small losses repeatedly. It is not at all obvious; of course, that the market goes in the desired direction the moment the trader has bought it. This case is even more the exception. The rule is therefore rather, that it first goes in the unwanted direction. The difficulty, of course, is to determine whether the trader is merely dealing with a temporary correction that should not be paid much attention to, or whether this is the beginning of a real turn in the market. No matter which of these cases occurs, the rule states: cut your losses. Therefore, the trend follower must close the position, whether or not he is right with his assessment.

According to my experience, a small group of people only performs such an iron discipline. Although the recommendation is based on correct observation and experience, it is difficult to carry out. This is also the reason why many trend followers have completely automated their system.

The computer then decides when to buy and sell. As important and correct this rule for trend followers might be, it is of little use in day trading or short-term trading. Since day trading is usually carried out based on a leveraged account, trend following is rarely useful here. If you plan to stay weeks or even months in a trade, the financing costs the broker will charge you will not stand in a reasonable ratio to the return.

The problems in day trading, which I am constantly discovering, are often the result of the fact that most traders have unfortunately borrowed their trading philosophy from the trend followers. Therefore, they are also trying to maximize their profits and minimize their losses. This sounds logical or rational, but it is difficult to carry out in day trading. If you study intraday charts, you will also see this. Often the market runs sideways for a few hours in a narrow range, and then shoots explosively upwards or downwards. This usually happens after important economic data has been published. You can clearly see that the market participants are just waiting for these data. Since it is uncertain, however, in which direction the move will occur, it is, of course, difficult to predict the direction of the price based on any analysis.

Many traders are also experiencing the fact that they have correctly assessed the market direction, but still lose their position, because the market first runs in the opposite direction and takes their stops out. This happens because their stops are so close to the market action, because they want to "limit their losses" according to the mantra of the trend followers. Eventually the many loss trades accumulate, and the few big profit trades are not big enough to make a profit at the end of the week.

Assertion 2: Try to Achieve a Good Risk Reward Ratio

The philosophy of the trend follower is most striking when it comes to the risk reward ratio (RRR). This is a number that tells how much a trader can (or is supposed to) risk achieving a certain return. Good trading, so the repeated mantra of most trading gurus, works with high RRRs. Therefore, you often see that a RRR of 1: 2 or even 1: 3 is required for short-term trading. Specifically, this means that if the trader risks 50 tics or pips (distance of the stop to the entry price), the price target should be at least 100 tics or pips. For example, if he buys the Dow Jones Future at a price of 18,000 points and puts a protective stop 50 points lower at 17.950, then the price target must be at least 18,100 points.

This means that a trader who bought the Dow at

18,000 points will have to hope that he will actually rise to 18,100 points in the next few hours. Maybe he really does. The reality, however, is often that before the good old Dow will do this favor for the trader he will first go back to 17.950 points again and get his stop out of the market. The Dow does not do this for bad reason to annoy the trader. He does this because markets simply work like this. The market tends to deceive the expectation of the trader. First.

As logical and mathematically correct the requirement of many trading gurus concerning risk reward ratios might be, the reality looks very different if the trader tries to trade this way. It is not easy to achieve a return of 100 pips or points with a risk of 50 pips or 50 points, however desirable. It becomes even more difficult, of course, if the gurus ask for RRRs of 1: 3 or even higher. Here you need higher magic to be successful.

Assertion 3: You Merely Need a Hit Rate of 33.33%

If the trader wants to meet the not quite immodest return of 100 points profit with a risk of 50 points, he would only need a hit rate of just a bit over 33.33% to trade profitably. Only 34% of his trades must reach the price target so that it can trade profitably so to say. At least this is what mathematics tells us. This requirement, too, sounds reasonable, of course. In addition, everyone who is confronted with this idea for the first time says: "Well, 33.33% I can do this! I can do it even better! "

The reality of trading is unfortunately quite different. Traders who enter the market with such premises are often exposed to a lack of volatility. The result is that the stated price target of 100 pips or 100 points is not reached at all (let alone 150 pips). The stop, however, which is only 50 points away from the entry price, is likely to be reached. The result is that the equation simply does not work. Mathematically, it is correct, but it is difficult to put it into practice. In addition, by the way, it does not matter if the trader works with a ratio of 30 - 60 or 20 - 40. The difficulties remain the same. The problem with this type of trading is, in my opinion, to be looked at in the underlying premise. This comes exactly from the already mentioned recommendation "cut your losses and let your profits run". At first glance, this recommendation sounds reasonable and rational, but it is not practical in the daily reality of short-term trading. Thus, it is clear that the failure is not due to the discipline of the trader (as so often asserted) but simply due to the wrong method. I would even go further and claim that it is due to the wrong trading philosophy. As advisable and true „cut your losses and let your profits run" might be for trend followers, this advice proves useless when trading short term.

More. My recommendation in this book is even going to be the opposite of what is recommended to the trend followers. My suggestion for intraday trading is actually: to keep profits as small as possible and to take big losses. As absurd as this recommendation sounds for some ears, it turns out being very effective when we test this proposal thoroughly and look at the results.

My recommendation when it comes to intraday trading is to try to trade as a scalper. Therefore, I prefer to realize permanently small profits but not to work with tight stops. If the day trader works with tight stops, he will experience that his position is constantly being stopped out. This is due to the nature of the markets, which are constantly succumbing to small fluctuations.

The price target of his position should therefore be selected as small as possible, so that it can be reached quickly and effortlessly. The stop, however, should be as far away as possible from the current price action. So far away, that under "normal market conditions" it cannot be reached at all. That this is going to happen anyway, speaks for itself. Market conditions and volatility are constantly changing. There will be occasional exaggerations, which, of course, will get stops that are waiting at levels that are far away from the present market.

The real idea of this strategy is that <u>the price target is achieved quickly and easily by the natural fluctuations of the market</u>. How fast this can happen, I will illustrate by means of several examples in the second part of this book. Important in this strategy is that you learn to understand that intraday trading is just not about making big profits. On the contrary. I want my price target to be reached as quickly as possible and then move on to the next trade. I therefore favor a chain of many small profits. This approach has many advantages. The most important of them in my opinion is **the fun factor**. If you win repeatedly, this motivates you enormously. Be honest. How do you prefer to earn your money: win once and lose five times? Alternatively, win nine times and lose once? I think the answer is obvious. Most people will choose the second variant. This is in human nature. That is why I am trying to develop a trading strategy that goes with human nature. It may seem more rational to opt for the first variant (which most trading books do). However, in practice it is difficult to carry it out. Believe me; I have tried it for years.

Most traders prefer to win always (or as often as possible). That is why I recommend that you look for a strategy that does exactly that: a strategy with the highest possible hit rate. With a few simple examples, we want to clarify how high the hit rate has to be, so that you ultimately can trade profitably. So if the trader is concentrating on steady small profits, he programs his way to trade (his brain) on this method. Since he always has steady small success, he stays motivated to continue. This is of enormous importance in trading. Trading is certainly a huge challenge. This is why steady success is very important. When experiencing little success, the trader quickly loses the motivation. **The second advantage** of small price targets is the reality of the market itself, which does not often give the opportunity to make big profits. He but always gives the opportunity to make small profits. That is why I favor this method, because I want a system that gives me lasting income. If you are on the hunt for big wins, you often have to wait for days until this anticipated movement of 100 points comes. In the course of time, my system might already get me 20 or 30 times 5 or 7 points out of the market.

In order for such a system with small price targets to be profitable, we naturally need a high hit rate. Because every now and then we will have a loss trade that will be reaping our profits. The high hit rate is the premise of this system. We need them and we want them. Moreover, it meets the natural need of human beings who always wants to win. You may regret this and even regard it as irrational, but working against human nature has always been one of the most difficult businesses. Therefore, we should not try it in the first place.

Part 2: A Trading Strategy with a Small Price Target

I would like to consider a simple trading strategy in terms of profitability using three back tests. In general, the trading literature places great emphasis on the strategy itself. Somewhere in every trader, there is a kind of graalseeker, who hopes one day to find the one secret strategy which none could discover so far. Maybe there exist such a strategy. Unfortunately, in my 15-year career as a trader I did not discover it anywhere. Any, but any strategy I have seen, traded or tested, had weaknesses, and major drawdowns.

Rather than focusing on the idle search for such an "infallible" strategy, I think it is much more fruitful to adjust the parameters of an existing strategy to enable us to reach our financial goals. In order for the trader to get an objective view of the performance potential of his chosen strategy, he should first test it. This, of course, he can do in a so-called demo account (paper trading). After one or two months, he should get an idea as to whether this strategy makes sense or not.

If, however, the trader wants to check the long-term profitability of a trading strategy, he should perform a **back test** for the set parameters. This is due to a special software that is now offered in many trading platforms. Therefore, usually you do not have to buy this software.

If you are back testing, you look at the historical data of a market in order to check the performance of your strategy with the chosen parameters. The results will make a statistical analysis possible with which the trader can assess the performance of his strategy. The premise of such a back test is, of course, the assumption that strategies that have worked well in the past have good chances to repeat this in the future. The same applies, of course, to strategies that have not performed well. As a rule, they will not do it in the future either.

Nevertheless, one should not forget that the past performance is not a guarantee for the future. When a trader tests a particular strategy, he wants to know whether the basic assumptions of his system work under certain market conditions. Not more but also not less. Back testing is therefore not perfect. However, the trader gets at least an idea what the strategy with the entered parameters in recent years would have performed, would he have been trading it.

Test 1: German Bund Future, Crossing Moving Average   Strategy

In order to keep it as simple as possible, I have decided to use a cross-moving average for my trading signals. This indicator is based on the intersection of a slow and a fast moving average. If the fast MA crosses, the slow MA from the bottom up, the system will only open long positions. Conversely, should the fast MA cross the slow MA from top to bottom, the system opens only short positions. I did a first test on the German Bund Future. The Bund, the German word for "bond," is a debt security issued by Germany's federal government, and it is the German equivalent of a U.S. Treasury bond.

Figure 2: Bund Future, 5-minute chart

As the setting for the crossing moving average, I chose 24, 51. The blue line (top) is the fast MA and the magenta line (down) is the slow MA. In this case, the blue MA was above the magenta MA. Thus, the system only opened long positions (arrows).

I set the price target to three tics, while the stop-loss order was 20 Tics.

Since the Bund Future was mostly in an upward trend for the selected period of the test (2006-2017), I also looked at the test results for long only. That is, in this case, I changed the parameters from long short to long only. Then the results of the test were displayed, if only long positions were traded. The results were, in fact, much better than if the system would have been trading the short side too. I strongly recommend that the trader make such minor changes to the tests. He will sometimes get surprising results. He will find out that some strategies are more effective in a given market if they are traded short only or long only. Long/short at the same time does not always give the optimal result.

In the above example of a particular trading day, the system opened ten long positions. The first nine trades mostly reached the target of three tics after less than 5 minutes. In this case, the strategy made 9 times 30 euros, thus 270 euros profit before fees. The green horizontal line above the candle represents the price target. In the case of the tenth trade, however, the market did not reach the price target. After a few hours, even the stop-loss order was triggered (red horizontal line below the candles, red arrow). In this case, the system generated a loss of 20 tics or 200 euros. The gross profit for this trading day was thus:

270 (9 x 30) - 200 (1 x 200) = 70 euros

Figure 3: Performance histogram, Bund-Future from 10.12.2016 to 3.1.2017

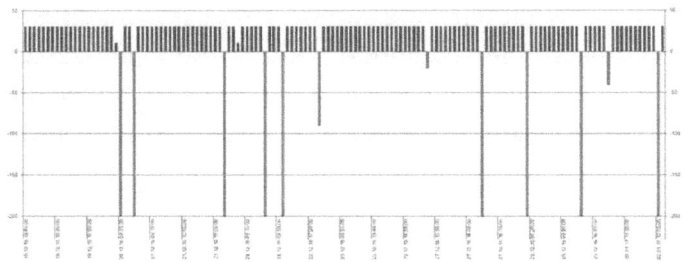

The performance histogram in Fig. 3 illustrates how the system operates. The small blue bars above represent the profit trades, while the red bars below symbolize the loss trades. As expected, the profit trades are clearly in the majority due to the small price target. The price target of three tics is usually achieved.

In the period from 10 December 2016 to 3 January 2017, however, the stop of 20 tics was reached nine times. However, there were also three loss trades where this was not the case. Here the system closed the position before the market reached the stop. Since it was a pure intraday trading strategy, I implemented a "block" in the system. This means that all open trades will be closed at 6:00 pm and no new trades will be opened. This measure is necessary in order to protect the performance from unnecessary losses due to gaps.

If I choose a price target of three ticks, this means that I want the target to be reached quickly and easily. In the above example, this has worked well in nine of the ten trades. Only at the tenth trade, I had to accept a loss. If the trader had traded the strategy fully automatically, the stop-loss order would have been triggered on the 10th trade.

If the trader acts semi-automatically, he could of course limit the loss as soon as it became clear that the trade does not work. Here, of course, a subjective component comes into play. When does the trader "know" that the trade does not work? This decision, especially since neither the target nor the stop has been reached, is of course at his discretion (experience).
However, the strategy is designed to ensure that the target is achieved quickly and easily, which in most

cases (usually 5 to 10 minutes) happens. If a trade has, still not reached the target price after 30 minutes and if the position, for example, is five tics in the minus, it is imperative that the trader thinks about limiting the loss. If you are a 3-tics collector in the Bund Future, it makes no sense to spend more than an hour looking at a trade that simply does not work.

If the trader manages to close such trades before the stop loss order is reached, he will be able to significantly increase his overall score. From time to time, a fast movement will trigger the stop-loss order. This cannot be prevented. Nevertheless, the results of a good semi-automatic trader generally look much better than what the fully automatic system does. The system, of course, continues to trade without consideration for the market.

If the trader does not want to take the time to trade himself, he can rely on another tool of automated risk management: the time stop. The advantage of the time-stop is that it closes a trade after a pre-entered period. For example, this might be 30 or 60 minutes. A time stop will, of course, also prevent the market to reach the target from time to time. However, he will often prevent the trade from going to the stop, an advantage a trader should think about.

Figure 4: Results back test Bund Future Crossing MA July 2006 - January 2017

total net profit:	124495.06
total # of trades:	29069
winning trades:	25200
losing trades:	3869
percent profitable:	86.69%
profit factor:	1.20
avg win/avg loss:	0.18
Avg trade (win & loss):	4.28
percent in the market:	28.92%
RegCoeff*100/StdDev Equity:	0.0000
gross profit:	756297.06
gross loss:	631802.00
largest winning trade:	250.00
avg winning trade:	30.01
avg # bars in winners:	3.26
largest losing trade:	290.00
avg losing trade:	163.30
avg # bars in losers:	12.09
max consecutive winners:	61
max consecutive losers:	5
Std.Dev. all trades:	69.96
Std.Dev. winning trades:	2.79
Std.Dev. losing trades:	65.78
max # shares/contracts:	1
max drawdown:	5301.66
Commission paid:	0.00
Expectancy:	0.0262
Expectancy Score:	0.0017
Happiness Factor:	25.50
Performance/Drawdown:	23.48
Expectation:	4.28
evaluation start:	18.07.06 Tue 08:00
evaluation stop:	03.01.17 Tue 19:00

I conducted a back test for the period 18 July 2006 to 3 January 2017, the result of which you see in figure 4. Overall, a gross profit of EUR 124,495.05

was achieved. Assuming that the system for the entire period was trading a single contract. To the trading costs, I come to speak immediately. During this time, 29,069 trades were carried out. This sounds like a lot, but on a trade period of 10 years this is about 15 trades per day. This frequency can be expected at the small price target so that one can also talk of a scalping system. Of this, 25,200 trades were wins. This corresponds to a hit rate of 86.89%. Only 3869 trades ended in a loss. As expected, the average profit trade was 30 euros. This corresponds exactly to three ticks profit in the Bund Future.

There were some exceptions. The largest profit trade was 250 euros or 25 ticks. This can be the result of a fast move where the take profit order was executed at a much better price than the trader originally intended. Sometimes slippage (worse or better order execution) also happens to the advantage of the trader.

The biggest loss trade was 290 euros, which is nine Tics more than the fixed stop loss of 20 Tics. Slippage can also occur in extreme movements in a liquid futures market such as Bund Futures. This is particularly the case with important economic news or notes from the central banks. If you decide to trade this strategy yourself, you should try not to hold positions near such important events.

Interesting is the average loss trade, which was 163.30. Thus, the stop-loss rate was not always reached. This figure is probably the most important in this analysis. If the trader manages to reduce it further, he could significantly increase the profitability of the strategy, since he does not have to worry about the winners (unlike most other strategies).

In addition, the number of profit series is gratifying. In this test, impressive 61 profit trades were recorded one after the other. This is precisely the strength of this approach. In contrast, the largest loss series was made only five consecutive loss trades. This seems to me to be feasible, especially if the trader manages to minimize these losses.

As already mentioned: no system comes out without drawdown phases. A drawdown represents the maximum cumulative loss within a given period. For example, a given system can earn 100% profit within one year. Within this period, however, there may well be "fluctuations". For example, the system could suffer 15% loss in July and August compared to the June level. In this case, you would be talking about a maximum drawdown of 15%. The trader or investor can then decide whether he can accept the order of magnitude of such temporary loss periods. If he cannot, he has either to abandon the trading system or change the risk parameters so that the percentage drawdown is smaller.

The maximum drawdown of euros 5301.66 seemed to be for me in the manageable range. In relation to the gross profit of 124,495 euros, it is almost negligible. This means that the trader would be in the fortunate position that the strategy would increase the account almost continuously without any significant setbacks. So far, the result of the back test could convince me. If I look at the profit factor, however, I find that this is only at 1.20. What does the profit factor say about a trading system? It is a statement of how much risk the trader is willing to take to achieve a certain return. How do we calculate the profit factor? Quite simply, you add the total profits and divide them by the total losses.

Profit factor = (sum of profits) / (sum of losses)

In our test, this would mean:

Profit factor = (756.297, 06) / (631.802) = 1.197

Although the system achieves profit (the factor is above one!), however, an above-average risk is needed to generate this profit. We risk over 600,000 euros to achieve only 756,297 euros gross profit, which is very high.

Of course, this unfavorable relationship has to do with the type of trading system I have chosen. Trading systems that are based on the trend-following philosophy usually achieve higher profit factors. Since our target price is very small, and the stop-loss is as far away as possible from the entry price, it seems as if we risk a lot to make a small profit. However, this is precisely the premise of our system, which takes seriously the psychological need of most traders to achieve fast and small profits.

In trader circles, however, a profit factor of more than two is always regarded as a mark of "good trading". It is clear that this can only be achieved with positive risk reward ratios of 1: 2 or 1: 3. In addition, the trader should also achieve an above-average hit rate. The fact that such ratios are achieved only in the rarest cases actually is often hidden.

As long as my system is profitable and continuously produces profits, I can live as a trader with a profit factor of 1.20. After all, it depends on what you expect from your system. Much more problematic in the back test seems to me the expectation per trade. This was quite low at 4.28. This figure tells us how much profit per trade we can expect in the longer term (here ten years). How do you calculate the expectation of a system?

Expectation: (hit rate x average profit per trade) - ((1- hit rate) x average loss per trade)

Expectation: 0, 87 * 30 euro - (1-0, 87) * 163 euro = 4, 91 euro

Depending on the calculation, I get an average profit between 4 and 5 euros, which I can expect with this strategy in the end. This is where the trading costs come into play. The cost per round turn in futures trading is currently between 4 and 5 euros for most brokers

For example, if the trader pays 4.40 euros (2.20 euros per transaction) per round turn and you has to pay a stock exchange fee of $ 1.17, he cannot trade profitably with this average trade or expectation of 4.91 euros. On the contrary, he will lose money. This means, in the plain text, that although our system looked so promising, we must realize that we cannot make a profit at this low expectation after deduction of costs.

Even if you find a broker that offers you very favorable terms (under $ 1 per transaction), you will find it hard to trade profitably at such an expectation. It is therefore essential that we increase the expectation of our system. Alternatively, we would have to look for another system. We want to investigate the first variant further, since we have not optimized our simple Crossing MA system. However, before we go over to the second test, let us look at the capital curve of the first test of our Bund Futures Crossing MA system.

Figure 5: Bund Future Crossing MA, Equity Curve 2006 - 2017

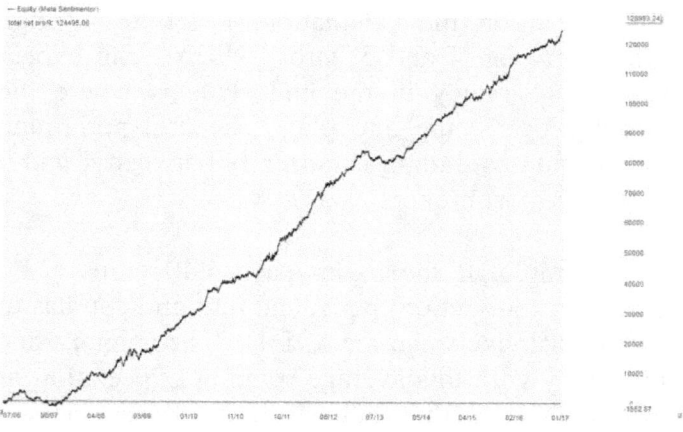

At first sight, the capital curve of our Bund Future system looks very good. There are hardly any significant setbacks, and the drawdowns, as already mentioned, are very limited. However, since this is a capital curve that stretches for 10 years, we have to find some difficulties on closer inspection. Thus the system needed at the beginning (bottom left) for over a year to get at all into the profitability. At the beginning, the team system drew a decent drawdown, which was financially unimportant, but still lasted over 12 months.

Even in 2013, the system could not achieve any appreciable profits and remained stuck at the 8000 Euro mark. This is not a broken leg, but which trader is able to trade his system disciplined for one year without earning a cent without twitching? So we also need a trading system here on a yearly basis, which promises us a profit at least, otherwise it could happen that the trader quickly passes the desire for his strategy.

Nevertheless, we would like to point out that such periods, in which a particular strategy does not make a profit are to be considered as normal. Trading is rare or never a one-way street. We can try to develop a strategy, which promises a profit on at least on a yearly basis. However, this cannot be guaranteed by any system. In terms of "income", trading is truly something that you must look at in the long term, which this capital curve clearly demonstrates.

Second test: E-Mini, Crossing Moving Average Strategy

Since I had not achieved the desired success in the

Bund Future, I now tried my luck in the E-Mini Future, the well-known Future on the SP500.

Figure 6: E-Mini, 5-minute chart

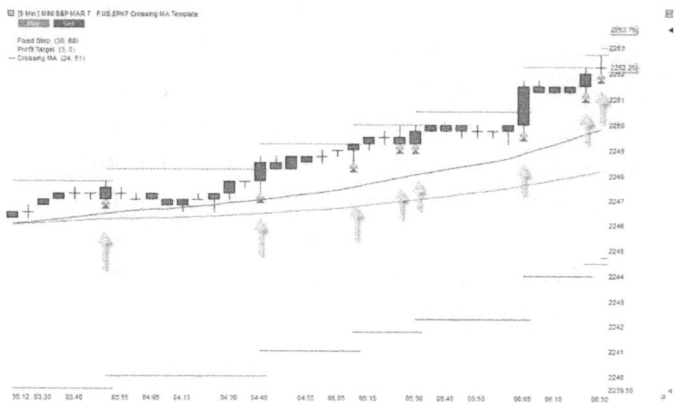

At the settings of the system, I changed only small things. The setting of the two moving averages I left to 24.51. I also chose a target of three tics for this test. However, I changed the stop. This I now put on 30 tics, which in the E-Mini usually means a proper distance to the current market. Here, too, I chose a long-only approach because the SP500 was also in an uptrend in the long term (as of January 2017). The probability that targets on the long side will be reached faster than on the short side, seemed to me to be bigger.

Figure 6 shows how the system works similarly to the Bund Future. The price target of three tics was reached relatively quickly with the first eight long trades (green arrows). If you consider the red horizontal lines below, you can see that on this trading day, none of these trades came close to the stops. The price target of three tics ($ 37.50 per traded contract), however, was usually achieved within 30 minutes.

Figure 7: Performance histogram 10.12.2016 - 30.12.2016

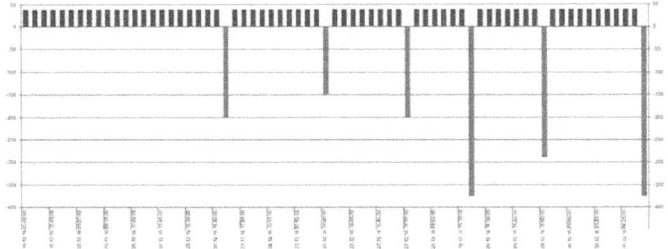

A similar picture is shown in the Bund-Future when we look at the performance histogram for a period of 3 weeks. Most trades reached the target and were winners (small blue bars above). There were nevertheless six loss trades during this period, of which only two reached the stop loss (corresponding to a loss of $ -375). The four smaller loss trades were terminated prematurely by the system.

Figure 8: Back test E-Mini, July 2011 – December 2016

total net profit:	86662.50
total # of trades:	16412
winning trades:	14776
losing trades:	1636
percent profitable:	90.03%
profit factor:	1.19
avg win/avg loss:	0.13
Avg trade (win & loss):	5.28
percent in the market:	45.77%
RegCoeff*100/StdDev Equity:	0.0000
gross profit:	554337.50
gross loss:	467675.00
largest winning trade:	225.00
avg winning trade:	37.52
avg # bars in winners:	8.45
largest losing trade:	375.00
avg losing trade:	285.86
avg # bars in losers:	31.83
max consecutive winners:	64
max consecutive losers:	4
Std.Dev. all trades:	106.22
Std.Dev. winning trades:	2.96
Std.Dev. losing trades:	137.64
max # shares/contracts:	1
max drawdown:	9062.50
Commission paid:	0.00
Expectancy:	0.0184
Expectancy Score:	0.0008
Happiness Factor:	10.63
Performance/Drawdown:	9.56
Expectation:	5.28
evaluation start:	13.07.11 Wed 00:00
evaluation stop:	30.12.16 Fri 22:55

The back test in the E-Mini was also positive. Since we only had data here until July 2011, we have only been able to carry out a test for the past 5 years. After all, the system carried out 16,412 trades during this period. Therefore, I consider this data statistically significant enough to give us an idea of this strategy in the E-Mini.

Overall, the system generated a profit of $ 86,662.50. There were 14,776 profitable trades and only 1636 loss trades. This corresponds to a hit rate of 90.03%. As expected, the average profit trade was close to the price target, namely $ 37.50. The average loss trade was significantly below the stop-loss threshold of $ 375 at $ 285.86. The largest loss trade was $ 375, which really speaks for this market. If the loss trades did not show slippage once, this indicates how deep the liquidity of this market is, which is why the E-Mini is so popular with traders.

After all, there were also here considerable profit series. The longest recorded 64 profit trades in a row. The longest loss series had only four trades. Again, this is very good data. The maximum drawdown with $ 9062.50 was slightly higher than in the Bund-Future, but with respect to the overall profit, you can live well with this result. The key figures profit factor and expectation already mentioned in the Bund Future test once again prepared me for a headache. These are similar here. The profit factor was also relatively weak at 1.19. In addition, the expectation or the average profit per trade is too low with $ 5.28 (arrow) to trade profitable. Therefore, I had to make some changes to the parameters if I wanted to trade the system profitably in the E-Mini. First, we look at the capital curve of this test.

Figure 9: E-Mini Equity Curve, 2011 - 2016

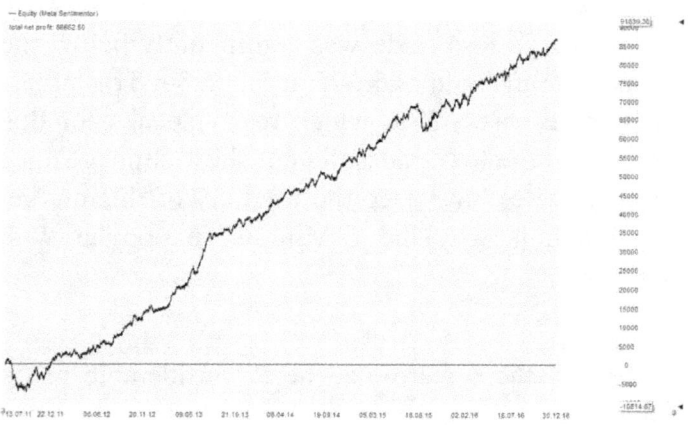

Here, too, the capital curve seems to go quite in the desired direction. As already mentioned the drawdowns were limited. Many traders would pre-draw for such a capital curve. Nevertheless, the system started in mid-July 2011 just with a drawdown (at the bottom left of the chart, the blue line is the zero line). Therefore, it took some months for the system to start making money. This clearly shows that drawdowns can occur at any time, even if you are just beginning to trade. In 2015, it happened again. However, the strategy was able to catch up the accumulated losses relatively quickly. As far as everything goes well.

Third Test: E-Mini, Crossing Moving Average Strategy with Adapted Parameters

In order to achieve a better result with the strategy, good trading software enables us to perform so-called optimizations for individual or all parameters of the system. For example, if I want to find out if I can get better results if I choose a slightly larger price target, the system can carry out a test with this changed target. For example, the system could find better results by choosing a profit target of five tics instead of three tics. The same applies, of course, to the stop or to the settings of the indicator, which gives the system the signals.

The back test itself, however, does not indicate the parameters with which our system generates the most stable results. If one is concerned with the optimization of trading systems, the danger of over-optimization, the so-called curve fitting (adapting parameters to the historical data set) lurks. A system that is strongly "curve-fitted" is seemingly optimally adapted to the data of the past, but usually fails as soon as one starts to trade it real time. The real question is, however, where does curve fitting actually starts? This is an ever-discussed topic for system developers. It is therefore hard to give a general answer. If you see an automatic trading system that seems almost too good to be true, you should be at least critical (especially if you have to pay a lot of money for it!). Unfortunately, many traders who bought a so-called black box, which promised them the blue of the sky, have had this experience. They soon had to realize that the system did not generate the promised return as it was on the packaging.

Since I do not intend to recommend the reader pure automatic trading in this book, I do not go deeper into this question. The decisive factor for me was to check whether I could improve the system with small optimizations. Remember it already shows a positive result without optimization at all. As mentioned several times, the crucial optimization is in the trader's ability to recognize and minimize the loss trades in time. If the trader succeeds, for example, to close 30% of these trades earlier, the desired outcome would be achieved. In a new test of the crossing MA system in the E-Mini-Future, I have changed two parameters. I have set the price target of the long positions from three to two tics. The critics of such a decision may argue that this is an extremely small price target for which the trading costs are no longer proportionate. I will invalidate this objection with a sober view of the data.

On the other hand, I set the stop in an almost inaccessible distance from the market, namely to 100 tics distance to the entrance. Again, this is a radical decision that can be criticized. If you only want to win 2 tics and risk 100 tics, you work with an extremely negative risk reward ratio. This decision is therefore the stark opposite of what is commonly recommended.

This last decision, of course, has far-reaching consequences. On the one hand, I hope that the stop is reached only in rare cases. If the stop is triggered, he causes a huge loss, namely $ 1237.50 per contract, which of course always pulls a tear through the capital curve. On the other hand, the real question is: how often would such an event occur, and what does it mean for the growth of my equity curve?

The only optimization that I have actually carried out from the system was related to the parameters of the cross-moving averages. So far I had used the setting 24, 51. After a test, however, it turned out that the setting of 42, 92 gives me the better results.

Figure 10: E-Mini, 5-minute chart

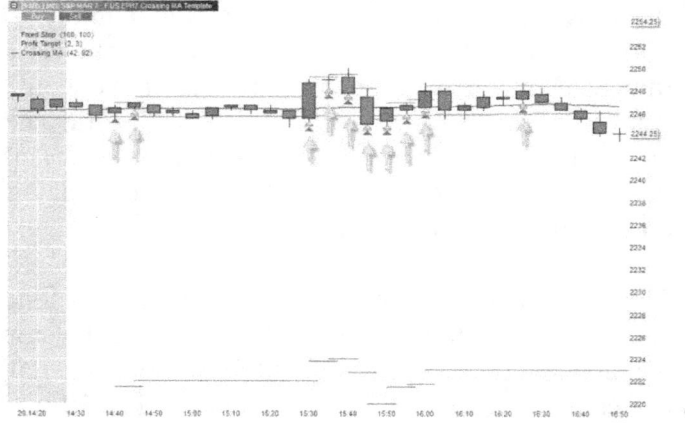

Here we see the optimized system at work. The red horizontal lines below are the respective waiting stop-loss orders that are at a safe distance from the price action. On the day I made this screenshot, none of those orders was triggered. Ten long positions (green arrows) were opened, of which the first nine reached the price target. The tenth long position was closed by the system at the end of the trading day with a loss of 23 Tics or $ 287.50. A loss of this magnitude would not have been necessary in my opinion. After all, the position remained open for an hour and a half, which is just too long for this strategy. A trader could close the position sooner and limit the loss. This will not always succeed, but repeatedly. Let us look at the winner/loser ratio on the performance histogram.

Figure 11: E-Mini, performance histogram 10 December 2016 - 4 January 2017

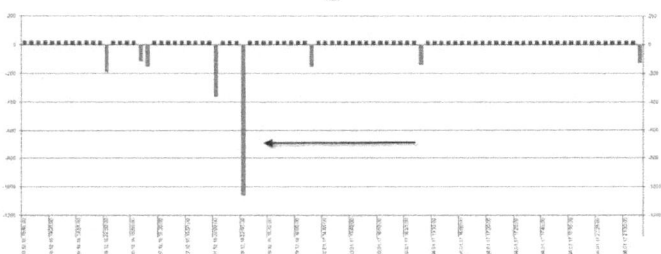

On the performance histogram from 10 December to 4 January 2017 we see exactly the problems mentioned. The vast majority of trades are winners as expected (blue bars above). The trader does not have to worry about this. All his skills would thus be reflected in the management of the loss trades. That is why we should look at the one big loss ($ 1062.50, arrow) from 28 December 2016.

Figure 12: Loss trade of 28 December 2016

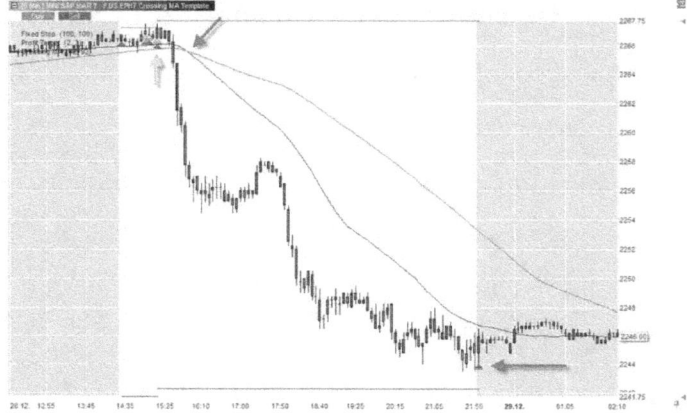

As seen clearly in the chart, the long position was opened in the early morning (early afternoon in Europe) of 28 December (green arrow left above). At the time, the market was still going sideways and some previous long trades were already successfully closed. Crucial for this trade seems to me that 15 minutes after the long position was opened the market suddenly broke down (red candles in the chart after the entry). In addition, the Crossing MA indicator changed from long to short. At the latest here, the trader would have had to intervene and close the position. He would have gotten away with a loss of $ 200-300 instead of $ 1062.50. Since a fully automated system could not assess such a situation, of course, it would have remain in the position until the close of trading. Since it was then closed with great loss (at the day low and only just above the stop loss order).

On the one hand, it is completely contrary to the philosophy of this strategy to hold a position over several hours, especially because the price target is very small. On the other hand, it would be bad risk management if a trader would not intervene. He MUST close such a position earlier to limit the damage. If he cannot do this, then it is indeed better to trade fully automatically and leave it to the computer how to act.

The only reason to act (semi-automatically) can only be that a trader can achieve better results than the fully automatic system. This example shows clearly that this is quite possible. Even limiting the damage to half (loss of $ 500) would significantly improve the overall result of the system. And that is where it is all about.

Figure 13: E-Mini, second back test 2011 - 2017

total net profit:	157250.00
total # of trades:	17144
winning trades:	16309
losing trades:	835
percent profitable:	95.13%
profit factor:	1.62
avg win/avg loss:	0.08
Avg trade (win & loss):	9.17 ⬅
percent in the market:	17.56%
RegCoeff*100/StdDev Equity:	0.0000
gross profit:	412362.50
gross loss:	255112.50
largest winning trade:	1225.00
avg winning trade:	25.28
avg # bars in winners:	2.56
largest losing trade:	1337.50
avg losing trade:	305.52
avg # bars in losers:	31.33
max consecutive winners:	129
max consecutive losers:	3
Std.Dev. all trades:	103.35
Std.Dev. winning trades:	11.21
Std.Dev. losing trades:	335.91
max # shares/contracts:	1
max drawdown:	5700.00
Commission paid:	0.00
Expectancy:	0.0298
Expectancy Score:	0.0013
Happiness Factor:	30.76
Performance/Drawdown:	27.59
Expectation:	9.17
evaluation start:	18.07.11 Mon 00:00
evaluation stop:	05.01.17 Thu 12:25

In this second back test with changed parameters, the system carried out 17,144 trades. Of this, 16,309 were profitable, which corresponds to a hit rate of 95.13%. The gross profit was $ 157,250.00. The average profit trade was $ 25.28 as expected. This is slightly higher than the target price of $ 25, which suggests some slippage to the advantage of the trader. The average loss trade was slightly higher at $ 305.52 than in the first test. The longest series of winners reached a spectacular 129 profit trades in a row. On the other hand, the longest loss series was only three trades long.

The maximum drawdown stayed with $ 5700 in the acceptable range. This time the profit factor was much higher: 1.62, which indicates that, in spite of the much higher stop-loss this system is much less risky than the previous one. This seems paradoxical; I risk 100 Tics to win only two Tics. Nevertheless, the test for this approach gives me a lower risk. Obviously, my assumption is true that one should put the stop as far away from the market as possible in order to be able to trade profitably. This is also a realization that does the opposite of what is commonly recommended in the trading literature. Finally, the system also achieved a satisfactory result in terms of average profit. At $ 9.17, the expected value was well above the result of the first test. Considering the small price target of 2 tics, which promises a maximum profit of $ 25 among the winners, this is a good result, which can be traded profitably even after costs deduction.

A key figure that I have not discussed so far is the so-called "average bars in winners", the number of 5-minute candles needed for the profit trades on average to reach the price target. For the profit trades, this is low as expected, namely 2.56 candles. This means that the profit trade needs an average of about 13 minutes to reach the goal. In the case of loss trades, the number looks quite different. On average, it lasted up to 31.33 candles until the loss trade was closed. That is about 2.5 hours. For the semi-automatic trader this is clearly too long. These data also show that the results can be clearly improved if the trader is able to intervene more quickly.

With regard to the money management, of course, every trader needs to decide how many contracts he can deal with such a strategy. If he has to accept losses of over $ 1000 every now and then, he would certainly need a higher five-digit sum to do so responsibly. If the trader succeeds in significantly reducing the loss trades, the strategy could be traded with smaller sums. To get a better idea of the possible drawdowns, let us look at the capital curve for this period.

Figure 14: E-Mini, second back test, Equity Curve 2011 - 2017

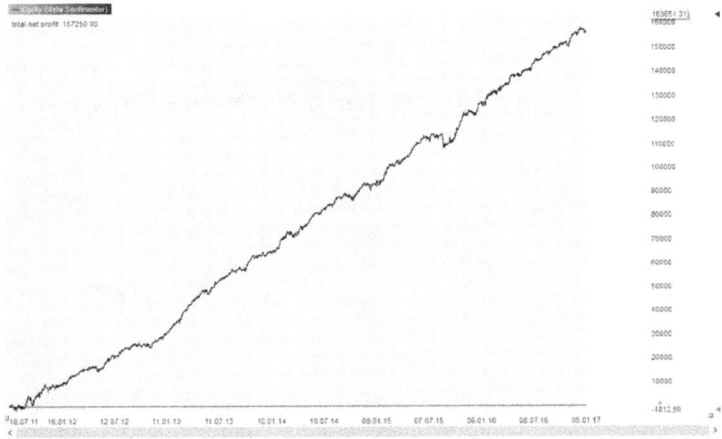

The equity curve now has a course which every trader would in principle always want. The drawdowns are small and are quickly caught up. I also looked at the little "buckle" in August 2015. Here, in fact, the stop was reached several times in succession, resulting in the loss of several thousands of dollars. Looking more closely at this period in the chart (between the 24th and the 28th of August 2015), this is exactly the time when a small crash took place in the American indices. I hope it is clear that a responsible trader would not have stuck in a long position five times in succession under such circumstances.

If any reader cannot really believe that you can develop a trading system with a hit rate of 95%, which is profitable in the long term, please look at the trades of 4 January 2017.

Figure 15: Trades of 4 January 2017

04.01.17 Wed 01:59	Long	1	2253.25	0.00		
04.01.17 Wed 02:09	close Long (Profit Target 2253.75)	1	2253.75	0.00	25.00	168212.50
04.01.17 Wed 02:09	Long	1	2253.75	0.00		
04.01.17 Wed 02:29	close Long (Profit Target 2254.25)	1	2254.25	0.00	25.00	168237.50
04.01.17 Wed 02:29	Long	1	2254.50	0.00		
04.01.17 Wed 04:44	close Long (Profit Target 2255.00)	1	2255.00	0.00	25.00	168262.50
04.01.17 Wed 04:44	Long	1	2255.25	0.00		
04.01.17 Wed 05:59	close Long (Profit Target 2255.75)	1	2255.75	0.00	25.00	168287.50
04.01.17 Wed 05:59	Long	1	2255.75	0.00		
04.01.17 Wed 10:49	close Long (Profit Target 2256.25)	1	2256.25	0.00	25.00	168312.50
04.01.17 Wed 10:49	Long	1	2255.75	0.00		
04.01.17 Wed 10:54	close Long (Profit Target 2256.25)	1	2256.25	0.00	25.00	168337.50
04.01.17 Wed 10:54	Long	1	2256.25	0.00		
04.01.17 Wed 10:59	close Long (Profit Target 2256.75)	1	2256.75	0.00	25.00	168362.50
04.01.17 Wed 10:59	Long	1	2255.75	0.00		
04.01.17 Wed 11:04	close Long (Profit Target 2256.25)	1	2256.25	0.00	25.00	168387.50
04.01.17 Wed 11:04	Long	1	2256.75	0.00		
04.01.17 Wed 13:59	close Long (Profit Target 2257.25)	1	2257.25	0.00	25.00	168412.50
04.01.17 Wed 13:59	Long	1	2257.25	0.00		
04.01.17 Wed 14:04	close Long (Profit Target 2257.75)	1	2257.75	0.00	25.00	168437.50
04.01.17 Wed 14:04	Long	1	2257.75	0.00		
04.01.17 Wed 14:19	close Long (Profit Target 2258.25)	1	2258.25	0.00	25.00	168462.50
04.01.17 Wed 14:19	Long	1	2258.00	0.00		
04.01.17 Wed 14:29	close Long (Profit Target 2258.50)	1	2258.50	0.00	25.00	168487.50
04.01.17 Wed 14:29	Long	1	2258.00	0.00		
04.01.17 Wed 15:34	close Long (Profit Target 2258.50)	1	2258.50	0.00	25.00	168512.50
04.01.17 Wed 15:34	Long	1	2261.50	0.00		
04.01.17 Wed 15:39	close Long (Profit Target 2262.00)	1	2262.00	0.00	25.00	168537.50
04.01.17 Wed 15:39	Long	1	2259.50	0.00		
04.01.17 Wed 15:44	close Long (Profit Target 2260.00)	1	2260.00	0.00	25.00	168562.50
04.01.17 Wed 15:44	Long	1	2259.50	0.00		
04.01.17 Wed 15:49	close Long (Profit Target 2260.00)	1	2260.00	0.00	25.00	168587.50
04.01.17 Wed 15:49	Long	1	2260.25	0.00		
04.01.17 Wed 15:54	close Long (Profit Target 2260.75)	1	2260.75	0.00	25.00	168612.50
04.01.17 Wed 15:54	Long	1	2261.50	0.00		
04.01.17 Wed 16:04	close Long (Profit Target 2262.00)	1	2262.00	0.00	25.00	168637.50
04.01.17 Wed 16:04	Long	1	2262.00	0.00		
04.01.17 Wed 16:09	close Long (Profit Target 2262.50)	1	2262.50	0.00	25.00	168662.50

This figure illustrates the advantages of this trading system. It usually wins with a great ease. This also happens without the trader.

Such a system solves exactly what I mean when I say that traders should only be active on the stock exchange for a reason: to collect as many tics, pips or points as possible in the shortest possible time. If a trader makes the effort to go to such a crazy place, then for no other reason than to make money: permanent, continuous and constant. It demonstrates that trader should not spend his time with endless analyzes. This may indeed satisfy his intellectual curiosity. However, it usually does not make him fill his pockets. I know that well-meaning traders or trading coaches claim to be disciplined, or to deal with trades with a high-risk reward ratio. On the other hand, however, very well founded scientific studies show that we only have a limited amount of willpower (discipline). If this limited amount is exhausted, we are very happy to be distracted and do not want what these coaches want us to do. You can compare it to a muscle whose strength gets less and less after training for a few minutes.

If traders use all their strength and concentration in the hunt for profits, there is not much left for the control of the losses. If on the other hand you let an automated system make your winning trades, you can instead devote yourself to managing the few loss trades. In addition, that is what it is all about when it comes to trading.

Conclusion

I have not published the presented strategy, so that the reader can take it and trade. It can be traded, fully automated or semi-automatic. In addition, back testing never guarantees that results obtained in the past can be achieved in the future. Every trader who tests strategies should always be aware of this: a test is a test. Not more but also not less. Although the results of the strategy are "good", this does not mean that each trader can achieve a similar return. Markets are constantly changing, and a trader's learning curve plays a decisive role in whether or not a given strategy is profitable. In this book, I was primarily concerned with examining certain claims most trading books make. I am aware that such a questioning of seemingly fixed knowledge is not always appealing and can provoke criticism. Then I would have reached my goal. What would be better than a dynamic trader scene, which is ready at any time to question itself and explore new trading horizons?

I wish you lots of success with your trading!

Heikin Ashi Trader

You can reach the author at the following e-mail address: pdevaere@ahoo.de

Glossary

Automated or algorithmic trading: Indicates the automatic trading of securities by computer programs.

Back test: Identifies the process of evaluating a strategy by applying historical data

Black box systems: computer programs that automate trading of securities whose parameters the user does not need to see or know to use the system

Break Even: Profit threshold

Broker: Financial service provider who is responsible for the execution of securities investors' orders

Bund Future: German Term contract, which refers to a notional, long-term German federal bond, with a coupon of 6 percent and a maturity of 10 years

Candlestick: Representation of price changes based on a Japanese analysis technique

Commissions: Costs incurred in the purchase and sale of securities or futures contracts

Continuation pattern: Pause in the main trend, at the end of which the previous direction is resumed

Crossing Moving Average: Strategy based on the intersection of two standard indicators (moving averages)

Curve fitting: Adaptation of parameters to the historical data set

DAX: German stock index

Day trading: Day trading describes the short-term

speculative trading of securities. Positions are opened and closed again within the same trading day, with the aim of benefiting from low price fluctuations

Discretionary trading: Trading approach based on subjective analysis processes of a trader

Drawdown: losses that can arise out of the peak within a certain time

E-Mini-Future: Futures contract on the American Index SP500

Entry strategy: A strategy that determines the entry into a market

Equity curve: Performance curve

Equity index: Indicator for the price performance of the equity market as a whole or individual equity groups (for example Dow Jones)

Eurostoxx50 Future: Future on the European stock index, which contains 50 large listed companies of the Eurozone

Exit strategy: A strategy that determines the exit from a market

Expectation: Indicates the average of the results when the experiment is repeated indefinitely

Forex: International foreign exchange market

Futures: Standardized contract for the purchase or sale of a certain quantity of goods, at a fixed price, on a certain date

Gap: Course gap between two trading days

Heikin Ashi Chart: Japanese: "Balancing on a Foot". Japanese representation of price changes
Hit ratio: Describes the ratio of profit trades to loss trades
Indicator: Indicator in technical analysis, which is used to determine price movements of securities
Learning curve: Describes the success rate of learning over the course of time in trading
Liquidity: Describes the extent to which a security can be bought and sold at any time
Long: To be long is to buy and hold securities

Long only: Parameter setting, which only opens long positions in the system
Long / Short: Parameter setting, which opens both long and short positions in the system
Mean-reversion: The tendency of a financial market to return to its average after an extreme position
Money management: A value-added strategy that aims at controlling the risk of a securities portfolio by setting the size of the individual trading positions
Moving average: Moving average, indicator
Optimization: Processes in applied mathematics, which attempts optimal parameters of a usually complex. System
Performance histogram: Performance measurement for a given trading period
Pip: Percentage in point, smallest change in price in foreign exchange trading
Price target: Stock market price, which a security is to reach as a result of an analysis
Profit factor: Figure that divides the gross profit by

the gross loss

Retracement: A temporary reversal that goes against the prevailing trend

Risk Management: Includes all measures for the systematic identification, analysis, assessment, monitoring and control of risks

Risk reward ratio (RRR): The RRR serves as an indicator of the meaningfulness of a trade. It is calculated by dividing the expected profitability by the greatest possible loss (stop loss)

Round turn: Completed transaction where a security has been bought and resold

Scalping: Trading technique, in which the trader tries to trade minimal movements in the market

Semi-automatic trading: Trading approach, where the trader makes trade decisions partly to an automated system, partly by hand

Short position: A trader is short when he sells a position without owning it (short sale)

Slippage: The difference between the intended price and the actual price for the purchase of securities

S & P 500 (Standard & Poor's 500): A stock index comprising 500 of the world's largest listed American companies

Stop loss order: Sales order, which is executed as soon as a certain price is reached

Take profit order: Automated stock exchange, triggered as soon as a predefined price target has been reached

Tic: Smallest price change on a futures market

Time Stop: This order automatically closes a position after a predefined number of periods

Trading range: Price area in which a market is traded in one specific time period (one day, one week, several months)

Trailing stop: Automatically traced stop-loss order

Trend following: Trading strategy, which is based on following a once identified trend

USD/JPY: Exchange rate between the US dollar and the Japanese yen

Volatility: Standard deviation. Indicates how much a price fluctuates

More Books by Heikin Ashi Trader

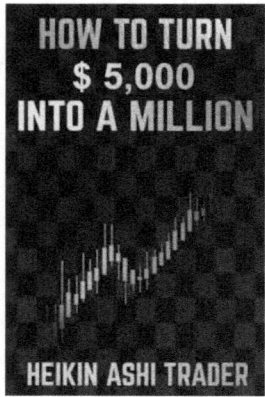

How to Turn $ 5,000 into a Million

Can you become a millionaire on the stock market? The question of how to grow a small account undoubtedly occupies every trader's mind. How do you manage to make a fortune out of a small amount? And preferably really fast?

Just as it is possible to build a real estate empire without a dollar of equity, so it is also possible to achieve high profits on the stock market with a small amount of starting capital (USD 5000 or less).

In this book, Heikin Ashi Trader presents a stock market strategy that will help the trader to succeed in this endeavor. Above all, he explains that the factor of position size plays a much more decisive role in trading success than is commonly assumed. The right question is not: how often are you right or wrong, but how big is your position if you are right?

This method is just about finding the markets where a significant movement can be expected. And once he has identified one, the trader should build a big position in that market, so that he can fully benefit from this movement.

Table of Contents

How to Trade a Range

Trade the Most Interesting Market in the World

Financial markets are predominantly trading in trendless zones, which traders call trading ranges or sideways markets. It then appears that they earn money when a market is in a trend and they should avoid trendless markets, because here there is nothing to write home about.

Despite this apparent finding, most short-term trading strategies rely on the trend-following model, although it is demonstrably difficult to implement. Most traders are more or less looking for a bigger move. The experience shows, however, that trading "moves" or "trends" is not that easy. Either the trader recognizes the trend too late, or the movement offers hardly any opportunities to enter.

There is, however, a specialized group of traders who do not care about trends. They do exactly the opposite. They trade when the market is in a range. This book describes the methods and tactics of these traders. It is not about how to identify a range and then to trade the outbreak from it, but how to trade the range itself.

Table of Contents

Trade Against the Trend!

The brokerage industry usually recommends that new traders trade with the trend. But is trading this way profitable? It is said that if you go with the trend, the likelihood that you will win is higher. Unfortunately, experience shows that most traders cannot build a profitable business this way.

Old and experienced traders used to say: You have to buy when blood flows in the streets. That means that you should act against the trend. Actually, this saying is the expression of common sense itself. The question remains: Why do traders find it so hard to put this wisdom into practice?

The new book by Heikin Ashi Trader gives ideas and tips on how to recognize such countertrend signals in the stock market, since these are usually the best trading opportunities.

Table of Contents

Part 1: The Snapback Trading Strategy

Part 2: Trading Examples

About the Author

Heikin Ashi Trader is recognized worldwide as the specialist in scalping with the Heikin Ashi chart. He has been trading this way for 19 years. He traded for a hedge fund and then went into business for himself as a trader. His scalping book "Scalping is Fun!" is an international bestseller and has been sold more than 30,000 times. You can find more information about his scalping method on his website www.heikinashitrader.net

With over 30,000 copies sold worldwide, the bestselling Heikin Ashi Trader book **"Scalping is Fun!"** is now an online course!

Discover how easy and fun scalping can be with the Heikin Ashi Trader method.

Skip the hassle of figuring out for yourself the fun way to trade. The "Scalping is Fun!" online course will help you enjoy scalping and be one step closer to financial freedom.

Join us in this course and avail yourself of the free workshop!

For more information, please visit:

www.scalpthemarkets.com